Original title:
Winter Tide

Copyright © 2024 Swan Charm
All rights reserved.

Author: Lan Donne
ISBN HARDBACK: 978-9916-79-912-3
ISBN PAPERBACK: 978-9916-79-913-0
ISBN EBOOK: 978-9916-79-914-7

The Secrets of the Frozen Forest

Underneath the icy trees,
Vows of silence dance with ease.
Shadows whisper ancient tales,
Of hidden paths where magic prevails.

Snowflakes fall like gentle sighs,
Veiling truths beneath the skies.
Branches cradle secrets deep,
In the forest where the stillness sleeps.

Echoes of Shimmering White

Whispers in the glistening snow,
Footprints lead where no one goes.
In the hush, the world stands still,
As frost's embrace enchants the hill.

A tranquil blanket, pure and bright,
Radiates the dazzling light.
Each shimmer tells a tale anew,
Of winter's grace in every hue.

Still Waters of Icebound Reflection

In the calm, the lake lies still,
Frozen heart, a timeless thrill.
Mirrored skies in crystal sheen,
Echo dreams of what has been.

Beneath the surface, secrets hide,
With every ripple, quiet pride.
Nature holds its breath to see,
The captured world, serene and free.

Frosted Whispers

In the air, a gentle chill,
Frosted whispers, soft and shrill.
Nature speaks in frosty breath,
A lullaby of life and death.

On the ground, the crystal lace,
Veils the world in pure embrace.
Every flake, a fleeting sigh,
Crafting moments passing by.

The Breath of Stillness

In the hush of twilight's grace,
Whispers dance in silent space.
Stars awake in softest glow,
Time stands still, the world moves slow.

Moonbeams weave through shadowed trees,
Gentle sighs in the evening breeze.
Nature's heart beats calm and slow,
In this moment, peace will grow.

Rippling streams in mirror night,
Echoes of a dreamer's flight.
Clouds drift by like thoughts untold,
Embracing stories, shy and bold.

With every breath, a world anew,
In stillness, find a vibrant view.
Hope ignites in darkest hours,
In silence bloom the hidden flowers.

So linger here, let worries cease,
In the breath of stillness, find your peace.
For every moment holds a song,
In quiet, we truly belong.

Frosty Visions

Morning light on icy lace,
Whispers of a frozen place.
Crystal dreams in frosted air,
Nature's beauty, so rare and fair.

Footsteps crunch on snow-kissed ground,
In the silence, magic found.
Trees adorned in winter's dress,
A peaceful scene, so full of finesse.

Stars twinkle in the chilly night,
Guiding hearts with gentle light.
Frosty breath in whispers low,
Secrets of the earth below.

Candles flicker in cozy nooks,
Stories shared in cherished books.
Outside, the world is white and bright,
Inside, warmth holds us tight.

So let the frost enchant your soul,
In its embrace, feel the whole.
Life's a canvas, pure and wide,
In frosty visions, let love abide.

A Whisper Among the Pines

Beneath the gentle trees,
Soft secrets float and sway.
A breeze through needles fleet,
Invites the heart to play.

Sunlight dapples green,
Nature's canvas so divine.
Footsteps hush on earth,
In this sacred space, we find.

The scent of pine lingers,
With wisdom carved in bark.
Each whisper tells a tale,
Of journeys yet to embark.

Shadows dance in twilight,
As twilight starts to fade.
A magic in the air,
In stillness, memories made.

Stars peek through the leaves,
As night embraces all.
In the quilt of darkness,
Nature's spirit calls.

Tranquility in White

Blankets of snow unfold,
Covering the world in peace.
Silent whispers in the cold,
Winter's breath, a sweet release.

Icicles drip like dreams,
Hanging from the eaves so bright.
The air is crisp and pure,
As day melts into night.

Footsteps crunch on frosted ground,
Echoes of a softer time.
In this hushed serenity,
Life feels like a gentle rhyme.

Moonlight kisses icy fields,
Where shadows softly glide.
Amidst the stillness found,
A heart can freely reside.

Nature's breath in white,
Calm envelops each stray thought.
In this winter wonderland,
A sanctuary is sought.

Essence of the North Wind

Through whispers of the trees,
The north wind sings its song.
A chill that sharpens senses,
Where wild spirits belong.

Clouds race across the sky,
In a dance of fleeting grace.
The world is alive with energy,
In this vast, open space.

Mountains wear white crowns,
As the wind shapes every crest.
Each gust tells of treasures,
In nature's endless quest.

Stars twinkle overhead,
Guided by the icy breeze.
In every gust we're reminded,
Of our place among the trees.

The essence of the wild,
Flows through every breath we take.
In every corner, every turn,
The heart of nature wakes.

Pale Reflections

In the stillness of dawn,
Light spills like honeyed gold.
Mirrors of the quiet lake,
Whisper stories untold.

Each ripple speaks of time,
Flowing gently, never fast.
A moment captured softly,
In reflections of the past.

Fog dances on the water,
A shroud of mystery drawn.
The world appears as shadow,
As light begins to yawn.

Bare branches arch above,
Their secrets intertwine.
In this place of solace,
The soul finds space to shine.

As daybreak breaks the quiet,
The world awakens slow.
In pale reflections resting,
A deeper wisdom flows.

Lanterns at the Edge of Frost

Glowing softly, lanterns sway,
In the chill where shadows play.
Whispers dance on frosty air,
Guiding dreams with tender care.

Beneath the stars, the night unfolds,
Stories in the warmth retold.
Each flicker, a silent song,
Binding hearts where they belong.

Crystals sparkle, moonlight beams,
Lighting paths for distant dreams.
Crisp whispers call the night to stay,
In the warmth, we'll find our way.

Through the grass, the frost will creep,
Where the secrets of night sleep.
Lanterns glowing, shadows cast,
Holding memories of the past.

So we gather, hand in hand,
In this cold, a promised land.
Night ignites with tales of yore,
Lanterns guide us evermore.

Resonance of the Ice Crystal

In the heart of winter's chill,
Ice crystals, bright and still.
Each a facet, light's embrace,
Nature's song in silent space.

Whispers echo through the trees,
Caught in crisp and frosty breeze.
Glistening like dreams untold,
Stories of the night unfold.

Moon above with silver hue,
Bathing earth in crystal blue.
Every sparkle, every gleam,
Holds the magic of a dream.

Beneath the stars, a canvas wide,
Where the dreams of ice reside.
Glowing softly, time stands still,
In this night, the world we fill.

Moments captured, fleeting glance,
In the stillness, heart's romance.
Resonance of winter's grace,
Echoed in this frozen space.

Frost's Silent Lullaby

Wrapped in silence, night descends,
Frosty breath, the world transcends.
Under stars with soft embrace,
Winter sings in gentle grace.

Crystal kisses touch the ground,
Nature's lullaby, profound.
Every flake, a whispered tune,
Swaying softly 'neath the moon.

Sleepy woods in twilight's guise,
Hear the melody that flies.
Branches whisper, leaves obey,
In this hush, the world will stay.

Frost paints patterns, pure and bright,
Embroidered by the silver light.
Wrapped in dreams, time drifts away,
In the magic, night will sway.

Close your eyes and drift with ease,
Let the night bring quiet peace.
Frost's soft lullaby will weave,
Comfort in what we believe.

Shivering Hearthside Tales

By the fire, warmth draws near,
Fireside tales, eager ear.
Crackling wood and glowing light,
Through the chill of winter's night.

Whispers tell of frost-born dreams,
Of silver streams and moonlit beams.
Each story, a cozy thread,
Weaving warmth where hearts are fed.

Tales of yore, adventures grand,
Echo through this hearthside band.
With every tale, the flames will dance,
Capturing hearts in a trance.

Laughter shared and voices raised,
In the glow, life's joys are praised.
Hand in hand, we brave the cold,
Amidst the stories, love unfolds.

As the frost outside us gleams,
Inside we're wrapped in woven dreams.
Shivering, we cherish all,
By the hearth, we're never small.

Beneath a Blanket of White

Snowflakes dance, soft and light,
Covering the earth, pure and bright.
Whispers of winter fill the air,
Nature sleeps without a care.

Trees stand tall in silent grace,
Adorned in white, a gentle lace.
Footprints trace a fleeting path,
Echoes of a child's laughter and math.

Icicles hang, gleaming and long,
A quiet world, a wintry song.
Frozen streams, a glassy sheen,
Reflecting beauty, calm and serene.

The sky dons a cloak of gray,
As daylight fades into ballet.
Stars peer down, shimmering bright,
Beneath this blanket of white.

In the hush, all worries cease,
A moment's pause, a breath of peace.
Winter whispers, soft and low,
Life's rhythms slow in falling snow.

The Shimmer of Stillness

Morning dew glistens like jewels,
Nature's canvas, rich and cool.
Silence reigns, a gentle pause,
Wrapped in beauty, we find cause.

Ponds reflect the sky so wide,
Mirroring dreams where secrets hide.
Gentle ripples break the calm,
A fleeting moment, a soothing balm.

Sunlight filters through the leaves,
Whispering tales that nature weaves.
Birds take flight in graceful arcs,
Painting the sky with joyful sparks.

The world holds its breath, it's true,
In the shimmer that shines anew.
Time slows down, its embrace divine,
In this stillness, the heart aligns.

Evening falls, the stars will wake,
In the quiet, dreams we make.
The shimmer of stillness will stay,
Guiding us on another day.

Echoes in Hibernation

The world is hushed, a soft retreat,
Where echoes linger, bittersweet.
Creatures nestled, dreams held tight,
Wrapped in shadows, out of sight.

Buried deep in layers of snow,
Nature whispers tales below.
Hearts beat slow in peaceful trance,
In this stillness, life's slow dance.

Moonlight spills on frosty ground,
In silence, ancient truths are found.
Each breath a story, held in time,
A symphony that rings in rhyme.

As seasons shift, the cycle spins,
The pulse of life beneath begins.
Awakening calls, a gentle shake,
Echoes in hibernation awake.

Spring will rise, a vibrant hymn,
All the world will sing again.
But for now, in slumber's hold,
Echoes of peace, a tale retold.

Celestial Chill

Stars above in velvet night,
A canvas of shimmering light.
Whispers of the cosmic dance,
Invite the heart to take a chance.

The moon, a pearl in dark expanse,
Casting spells that make us glance.
Frosty breath, a quiet thrill,
Wrapped in wonder, we stand still.

Galaxies swirl in silent hues,
Mysterious paths that we peruse.
Each twinkle, a wish that's set free,
In this chill, we long to be.

Nature breathes, a cosmic sigh,
Beneath the vast and open sky.
Dreams take flight on wings of night,
Celestial chill ignites our light.

As dawn approaches, colors blend,
The stars will fade but never end.
In this moment, we embrace,
The magic of the night's sweet grace.

Radiant Snowflakes

Glistening down from the sky,
Each flake a dance in the light,
Whispers of winter up high,
A frosty, magical sight.

Silent secrets they share,
Drifting softly, unaware,
Painting the world pure and bright,
Radiance in the night.

Each a unique little form,
Twisting, turning in the storm,
Charmed by the breath of the breeze,
Nature's art that aims to please.

Gathered on branches and eaves,
A canvas that nature weaves,
Transforming the earth's every hue,
Snowflakes dazzle, fresh and new.

In this season's embrace so tight,
Every flake brings pure delight,
A wonderland we dream to see,
Radiant snowflakes, wild and free.

Season of Longing

Beneath the stars we wait and yearn,
The sun has set, the candles burn,
Chill in the air, warmth in our hearts,
In dreams of spring, a longing starts.

Echoes of laughter from days gone by,
Memories drift like clouds in the sky,
Pulling us back to a time so sweet,
In every whisper, we softly meet.

Distant horizons call us near,
Fading wishes, a soft, sweet tear,
The world is quiet, wrapped in night,
In this season, all feels right.

Frosty footsteps crunching slow,
Through the stillness, the soft winds blow,
Every moment, a chance to reflect,
In this longing, we find what's perfect.

Hope flickers on in the dark,
An ember's glow, a tiny spark,
For in the depth of winter's grip,
Love and dreams will never slip.

Muffled Murmurs

In the hush of falling snow,
Voices whisper soft and low,
Secrets shared in winter's dream,
A world paused in a silver gleam.

Footsteps vanish, sounds subdued,
Nature draped in a tranquil mood,
While shadows dance in twilight's hold,
Muffled echoes, untold stories unfold.

Beneath the blanket, life takes pause,
Savoring stillness without cause,
Moments captured in a gentle sigh,
As time drifts on, we wonder why.

Underneath the moon's soft gaze,
In winter's embrace, we lose our ways,
Murmurs linger in the cold night air,
Painting the silence with tender care.

In this realm where dreams reside,
Where every whisper is amplified,
The world, a canvas, wrapped in light,
Muffled murmurs, pure delight.

A Tapestry of Frost

Threads of ice weave through the trees,
A stunning sight that aims to please,
Nature's craftsmanship unfolds,
In every pattern, a story told.

Delicate lace adorns the ground,
In every corner, beauty found,
Sparkling under the morning sun,
A tapestry where light has spun.

Frosted windows, a fleeting view,
Artistry crafted from the dew,
Each frosty breath a whispered vow,
In winter's cloak, we wonder how.

Winding paths, a frosty lace,
Each step taken, a gentle grace,
A symphony of cold and warm,
In this season, we gather and swarm.

As the dawn breaks, softly cast,
This tapestry shall never last,
Yet in our hearts, it will remain,
A frosted memory, sweet refrain.

The Breath of Frost

In winter's grasp the world is still,
Whispers of chill dance on the hill.
Each breath released, a cloud takes flight,
A shimmered dream in the pale moonlight.

Frosted branches, diamonds bright,
Nature holds her breath at night.
A symphony of silence sings,
In this realm where the cold wind clings.

The air is crisp, a gentle bite,
As shadows play in the soft twilight.
Footprints mark the story's end,
Each step a tale the winter sends.

Beneath the stars, the earth does gleam,
A frozen world, a whispered dream.
Time wanders slow, a fleeting guest,
In the cold embrace, we find our rest.

Soothed by the Silence

In a world where noise is loud,
I seek the calm away from the crowd.
Whispers quiet in twilight's fold,
A sanctuary where peace unfolds.

The gentle rustle of the leaves,
Nature hums, and my heart believes.
Warm sunlight dapples on the ground,
Soothed by the silence, love is found.

In hidden nooks where shadows play,
I listen close to what they say.
Secrets linger in the air,
Softly woven, beyond compare.

The clock unwinds, time drifts away,
In stillness, worries cease to stay.
Wrapped in quiet, I feel anew,
The world fades, all that's left is you.

Nightfall in Wonderland

As the sun dips low, the stars appear,
Whispers of magic linger near.
Shadows stretch, the dark unfolds,
A canvas where the night time scolds.

In wonderland, the fairies play,
Casting glimmers to light the way.
Moonlit paths invite the lost,
Through dreams we wander, no matter the cost.

A lullaby of crickets sings,
While time unfurls its silver wings.
Each gaze a spark, every sigh a start,
In the heart of night, we are set apart.

Beneath the trees, with branches wide,
The mystery of dreams does slide.
In night's embrace, our worries go,
As wonder stirs and hopes do grow.

The Lantern's Glow

In the twilight, shadows creep,
A flickering light begins to leap.
The lantern's glow, warm and bright,
A guiding star in the quiet night.

Through tangled woods, I gently tread,
Each step is soft, where dreams are fed.
The golden light breaks through the dark,
Illuminating paths that spark.

As secrets linger in the air,
The lantern shares its gentle care.
Hope ignites with every flame,
In this journey, we're not the same.

A beacon calling out with grace,
Finding home in this sacred space.
Together, we embrace the glow,
With every flicker, love will flow.

Solstice Shadows

Beneath the moon's soft glow,
The world is calm and still,
Shadows stretch and flow,
Whispers of the night are chill.

Fires crackle bright and warm,
Gathered in circles tight,
Stories weave a cozy charm,
Embracing winter's night.

Trees stand tall and proud,
Their silhouettes take flight,
Wrapped in a silver shroud,
Dancing with the night's delight.

Stars twinkle high above,
Like secrets in the skies,
Filling hearts with love,
As darkness slowly flies.

In the quiet of the hour,
Nature holds her breath,
In this sacred, quiet power,
Life begins anew from death.

Lanterns in the Snow

Lanterns light the path we tread,
Casting warmth in frosty air,
Each flicker whispers what's unsaid,
A glow that holds us in its care.

Snowflakes dance from skies above,
Landing soft on frozen ground,
Each one a note, a song of love,
In silence, magic can be found.

Footprints trail where dreams have walked,
Leading to a cozy space,
In the air, sweet laughter talked,
Moments shared in this embrace.

Beneath the stars, all hearts ignite,
As lanterns float to skies anew,
Each wish ascends into the night,
A promise held in every view.

Winter's touch gives life a pause,
In darkness, hope begins to grow,
With every lantern, every cause,
Our spirits shine like fires in snow.

Secrets Beneath the Cold

Beneath the blanket of the frost,
Lies the world, a whispered sound,
Dreams lie deep, at what a cost,
In silence, magic can be found.

The rivers sleep, their voices hushed,
While trees wear coats of white,
In the night, the stars are brushed,
With stories hidden from our sight.

Snow rests heavy on each branch,
Cradling secrets in the fold,
In every flake, a fleeting chance,
Of tales that time has yet to hold.

Frosty breath dances in the air,
Awakening the stillness near,
As if nature holds a prayer,
For springtime to draw ever clear.

In winter's grip, the heart stands still,
Waiting for the thaw's sweet kiss,
To draw back layers, quiet thrill,
And find the warmth in what we miss.

The Dance of Flurries

Flurries twirl and spin around,
A ballet of the winter's grace,
In their chaos, beauty found,
Each one leaves a fleeting trace.

Swirling winds begin to play,
Crafting patterns in the air,
As daylight softly slips away,
The world transformed, beyond compare.

Children laugh as snowflakes fall,
Chasing dreams in white delight,
With every leap, we break the thrall,
And dance beneath the dusky light.

A hush envelops all we know,
As twinkling stars begin to gleam,
This fleeting wonder starts to glow,
Embodied in a snowflake's dream.

In the evening's cooling breath,
Life's a dance of soft embrace,
Life's fleeting, yet defying death,
In flurries, we find our place.

A Distant Warmth

In the twilight glow, secrets hide,
Whispers of hope on the evening tide.
Stars flicker gently, a soft embrace,
Binding the night with a tender grace.

The moon drapes silver on restless seas,
Carrying dreams like the softest breeze.
Fading shadows where memories dwell,
Echoing stories only time can tell.

Embers flicker in the silent dark,
A distant warmth ignites the spark.
Every heartbeat a melody, sweet,
Drawing us closer, where souls will meet.

The Time of Long Shadows

When daylight wanes and shadows grow tall,
The world transforms, a quiet call.
Moments linger in the amber light,
Time whispers softly, fades into night.

Branches reach out like fingers of grace,
Holding the sky in a soft embrace.
Colors deepen, the horizon glows,
In the stillness, a secret flows.

Footsteps echo on the winding trails,
Stories of journeys, vast as the gales.
With every twilight, we pause and reflect,
On the paths we've chosen, the lives we connect.

Patterns in the Snow

Falling softly, white feathers descend,
A canvas of silence, where visions blend.
Each flake a story, unique to its plight,
Creating a tapestry, pure and bright.

Children laugh as they dance in the flakes,
Building their dreams with the joy that it makes.
Footprints linger on a winter's path,
Tracing the journey of love and of laughs.

Under moonlight, the landscape awakes,
A shimmering blanket that gently quakes.
Patterns emerge in the still, frosty air,
Nature's own art, crafted with care.

Mosaics of Ice

Where rivers freeze, their secrets lie,
Glittering fragments beneath the sky.
Shattered reflections in hues of blue,
Mosaics of ice, a wondrous view.

Winter's breath creates intricate design,
Nature's own brush, a force so divine.
Each crystal unique, with stories to share,
Whispers of seasons that linger and care.

Beneath the chill, life pulses and hums,
Waiting for warmth when the springtime comes.
Yet in this stillness, beauty ignites,
A fleeting moment in the heart of the nights.

A Canvas of Frost

Morning light dances bright,
A canvas dressed in white.
Every branch a sparkling gem,
Nature's art, a quiet hymn.

Whispers of the winter breeze,
Paint the world with gentle ease.
Footprints trail the silent ground,
In this beauty, peace is found.

Expanses stretch, so vast, so wide,
Where winter's secrets choose to hide.
A moment caught, eternally,
Frozen here for us to see.

Softly falls the crystal snow,
Covering the earth below.
In the stillness, heartbeats sync,
A tranquil space for us to think.

Each flake unique like fleeting time,
In this quiet, life will rhyme.
Wrapped in layers, warm and sweet,
A canvas of frost beneath our feet.

Stories in Snowdrifts

Snowdrifts tell of a day long gone,
Each tells tales as they weigh on.
Silent echoes of laughter shared,
In moments frozen, hearts laid bare.

Underneath a winter sky,
Dreams are caught as they drift by.
In every mound, a memory lies,
Whispers soft as the wind sighs.

Children play in snowy realms,
Imagination at the helm.
Building castles, knights intend,
Where every journey seems to blend.

Footprints lead to hidden trails,
Where stories linger, never pale.
In the white, a world unfurled,
A tapestry of winter's world.

As the evening softly glows,
In twilight's embrace, magic flows.
Stories nestled in each drift,
A treasure trove, a timeless gift.

Drawn by the Quiet

In the hush of falling snow,
Time slows down, whispers flow.
Nature wraps the earth so tight,
Drawing breath in soft twilight.

Frosty windows, a canvas bright,
Captured moments, pure delight.
A world transformed, colors fade,
In gentle tones, silence laid.

Winds caress the barren trees,
Glistening with every breeze.
Covered paths of muted sound,
In stillness, solace is found.

Stars peek through the velvet night,
Guiding dreams with twinkling light.
In the quiet, hearts align,
Connected by the sacred sign.

Each flake falls like whispers heard,
In the stillness, life is stirred.
Drawn together, night and day,
In the quiet, we find our way.

The Frost-Bitten Heart

In the chill of winter's breath,
Lingers thoughts of love and death.
A heart once warm, now turned to ice,
In the frost, a hidden price.

Tales of yearning, lost and found,
Echo softly, profound.
As frozen tears kiss the ground,
In the silence, hope unbound.

Through the shadows, dreams remain,
A flicker warm amid the pain.
Where passion burns, the heart ignites,
In the frost, the soul unites.

Beneath the layers, warmth survives,
Battling through as love contrives.
Weaving comfort in the cold,
A frosted heart, yet still bold.

Winter's chill may seize the night,
But a spark within ignites.
The frost-bitten heart will mend,
In love's embrace, let it transcend.

Shards of Icicle Light

Glistening edges hang so bright,
Reflecting the moon's soft light.
Each a story, sharp and clear,
Nature's jewels, so pure, so dear.

Fragile yet fierce, they dare to stay,
Melting dreams in the sun's warm ray.
Spring whispers close, the end draws near,
Yet they shimmer, with beauty sheer.

Underneath winter's heavy cloak,
Their silent music softly spoke.
A dance of beauty, fleeting, rare,
In the stillness, a wishful prayer.

Morning light begins to creep,
Secrets of night, they safely keep.
Shards of icicle, clear and bright,
Fade away in morning light.

Hearthside Reflections

Flames flicker in the cozy room,
Casting shadows that gently loom.
With each crackle, memories unfold,
Tales of warmth and love retold.

The smell of pine, a tender scent,
Wrapped in blankets, time is spent.
With friends gathered, laughter swells,
In the heart, the spirit dwells.

Each glow a moment cherished deep,
In the hearth's embrace, secrets keep.
Outside, the storm may roar and fight,
But here we bask in soft, warm light.

Reflections dance upon the wall,
As year's end comes, we heed the call.
To hold each memory, precious, bright,
In the haven of our hearthside night.

Embrace of the Snowbound

Silent whispers fill the air,
Snowflakes drift without a care.
Blankets white cover the ground,
In this stillness, peace is found.

Trees wear crowns of crystal white,
Guardians of the tranquil night.
Each branch bows under winter's grace,
Nature's pure and soft embrace.

Footprints trace a lone path wide,
Through the forests, side by side.
In the hush, we find our way,
Underneath the soft, gray sway.

Hearts grow warm in frosty air,
Together, nothing can compare.
In the snowbound world we roam,
With each breath, we feel at home.

Whispers of the Northern Wind

Across the pines, the cold winds sigh,
Carrying tales of days gone by.
Hushed secrets from the frozen earth,
In their breath lies winter's worth.

Howling through the night so clear,
Each gust a pulse, we hold so dear.
With every turn, they twist and bend,
A song of nature, without end.

Dancing through the barren trees,
Singing softly with the breeze.
Frosty touches on our skin,
A reminder of where we've been.

In the dark, their echoes call,
In the silence, we hear it all.
The northern wind, a guiding light,
In its whispers, we find our flight.

Glacial Borders of Time

Upon the edge of frozen lands,
Moments linger, tied by strands.
Whispers echo through the ice,
Time stands still, a cold device.

Crystals forming, sharp and bright,
Reflections dance in pale moonlight.
Each breath exhaled, a fleeting trace,
Caught in nature's timeless grace.

Mountains rise, their shadows cast,
Guardians of a distant past.
Silent stories, carved in stone,
Speak of ages long since flown.

Snowflakes drift, they swirl and twirl,
As if they weave a soft pearl.
In this quiet, secrets lie,
Beneath the vast and starlit sky.

A world untouched by human hands,
Echoes of life's softer strands.
In glacial borders, hear the chime,
Of nature's breath, the clock of time.

The Art of White Stillness

In the hush of winter's breath,
A canvas white, devoid of death.
Softly falling, pure and clear,
Nature's silence draws us near.

Trees adorned in crystal lace,
Every branch, a sculpted grace.
Beneath the cloak of chilly air,
Life pauses in this frozen lair.

Footprints trace forgotten paths,
Through powdery, untouched baths.
Stillness hangs, a sacred thread,
Where dreams and whispers softly tread.

Glistening fields under the sun,
Highlight what this world has spun.
In every flake, a tale is spun,
Of peaceful nights when day is done.

The art of white, serene and bold,
Speaks of warmth when nights grow cold.
In stillness, find a deeper way,
To greet the dawn of each new day.

Fragments of a Hushed World

Rustling leaves in muted tones,
Speak of hearts, and silent groans.
Each whisper floats on gentle breeze,
Cradling secrets 'neath the trees.

Fleeting moments, soft and shy,
Flee like shadows under sky.
In the still, we find our peace,
And let burdens slowly cease.

The world, it breathes a quiet prayer,
In every corner, dark and rare.
Fragments gathered, held in light,
Painting shadows of the night.

Echoes linger, soft and warm,
Creating calm amidst the storm.
In hushed tones, our dreams take flight,
Weaving futures out of night.

A tapestry of silent grace,
Each thread a soft embrace.
In fragments found and stories spun,
A whispered truth—become as one.

Frost's Tapestry Unraveled

Each dawn reveals a frosted veil,
Nature's art—a whispered tale.
Delicate threads of silver shine,
Binding elements, divine.

Beneath the frost, life softly breathes,
In fields where sunlight weaves.
Every pattern, sharp and true,
Speaks of worlds forever new.

Crystalline splendors catch the eye,
Embroidered skies where dreams may fly.
The chill of air, both sharp and sweet,
Draws us closer to our feet.

Footsteps crunch through snowy dreams,
As dawn spills forth in golden beams.
In the stillness, hearts unravel,
Lost in paths that gently travel.

A tapestry of frost, unique,
In each winter's breath we seek.
To know the beauty all around,
In nature's quiet, we are found.

Glacial Beauty

In the stillness, ice does gleam,
A world untouched, a frozen dream.
Shimmers whispered in the night,
Awakening soft, silver light.

Mountains tall in frosted grace,
Nature's canvas, a tranquil space.
Glaciers carve the earth so slow,
In their depth, wild rivers flow.

Beneath a veil of crystal glow,
Secrets lie in the depths below.
A symphony of winter's breath,
Echoing tales of life and death.

Stars above in silence gleam,
Painting shadows, a radiant theme.
In each flake, a story spun,
Of ancient journeys never done.

Time stands still, in nature's arms,
Wrapped in winter's tender charms.
Glacial beauty, pure and bright,
Awake the heart in quiet night.

Icy Reverie

Whispers dance upon the freeze,
In the hush, the heart finds ease.
Frosted branches, a lacework weave,
In this moment, I believe.

Silvery moon in the night sky,
Sprinkling dreams as the hours lie.
Every glint, a tale refined,
A treasure for the soul to find.

Frozen paths beneath my feet,
Echoes of a world discreet.
In the shadows, secrets wait,
I tread softly, contemplate.

Crystal landscapes call my name,
In their beauty, I find flame.
A reverie in icy bounds,
Life's still pulse in winter sounds.

In every drift of snow that flows,
A quiet song, the spirit knows.
Icy reverie, soothing grace,
In this stillness, I embrace.

The Dream of Snow

Softly, softly, the snowflakes fall,
Blanketing whispers, a gentle call.
In their silence, dreams take flight,
Carried afar on a cloak of white.

Each flake unique, a fleeting kiss,
In this pure world, I find my bliss.
Land untouched by the passing haste,
As if time paused, not gone to waste.

Underneath a star-studded dome,
In this magic, I feel at home.
The dream of snow, a lullaby,
Softly singing as the night drifts by.

Snow-laden trees, a wondrous sight,
Silent guardians, cloaked in light.
In every flurry, joy ignites,
A crystalline dance in winter nights.

With every breath, I taste the cold,
Stories of winter silently told.
The dream of snow, forever pure,
A fleeting moment, a heart's allure.

Midnight in the Frozen Woods

Midnight cloaked in frozen breath,
In the woods, a dance with death.
Silent shadows weave and twine,
Underneath the stars that shine.

Crystalline branches shimmer bright,
Embraced by the embrace of night.
The moonlight guides my wandering ways,
Through the stillness, where magic plays.

Footfalls muffled, whispers low,
In the heart of winter's glow.
Every corner holds a secret hand,
In the silence, I understand.

Frozen echoes, a ghostly song,
Carving paths where dreams belong.
Midnight's spell wraps like a shawl,
In this stillness, I feel it all.

In the woods, my spirit roams,
Among the trees that call me home.
Midnight in the frozen woods,
Where nature sings, and silence broods.

Frost's Gentle Caress

A whispering chill in the air,
Dewdrops cling to blades with care.
Moonlight dances on silver streams,
Frosty moments, woven dreams.

Crystals form on each branch tip,
Nature's beauty, a gentle grip.
Softly glistening in the dawn,
A fleeting spell, almost gone.

In silence, the world seems to pause,
Wrapped in winter's soft applause.
Each breath a cloud, white and light,
As if dreams take wing at night.

A blanket of white on the ground,
In this stillness, peace is found.
With every step, a crunching sound,
While the frosty dusk surrounds.

Embraced by winter's tender kiss,
A symphony of chill and bliss.
Frost's gentle touch, a fleeting gift,
A quiet moment, spirits lift.

A Breath of the North

A cold wind blows from distant lands,
Whipping 'round the ancient strands.
Whispers echo through the trees,
Carried forth by frigid breeze.

Pine and cedar bend and sway,
Caught in nature's wild ballet.
The sky turns gray, a solemn hue,
Hints of snow are slipping through.

Mountains stand with regal grace,
Veiled in white, they find their space.
A crackling fire, warmth in sight,
Against the chill of the night.

Inhale deep the winter air,
Feel the lively pulse laid bare.
A breath of tales from ages past,
Carried forth, forever cast.

In the hush, the world can hear,
Nature's secrets, brave and clear.
A call to wander, roam and seek,
In the heart, the wild is meek.

Threads of Ice

Delicate threads of crystal lace,
Whirling softly in frosty space.
Nature's art in realms both wide,
Harmonies in winter's stride.

Beneath the sky, a canvas bright,
Stitched with stars in the quiet night.
Every flake a story told,
In shimmering white, their fate unfolds.

Across the lake, the breath of frost,
Nature's dance, never lost.
Echoes linger, soft and sweet,
Tread lightly in this serene retreat.

Whispers of magic in the air,
Crisp and clear, beyond compare.
Each moment woven, threads entwined,
A tapestry by nature designed.

In the stillness, find your way,
Follow whispers of winter's play.
Threads of ice, both soft and bold,
In every heart, their magic holds.

The Stillness of Night

In the heart of darkness deep,
Silence blankets all in sleep.
Stars above, a watchful gaze,
Guide the dreams of those who wander maze.

Snowflakes drift like whispered sighs,
Carrying secrets through darkened skies.
Each soft flurry tells a tale,
Of moonlit nights and winds that sail.

The world lies wrapped in peace tonight,
Embraced by velvet, soft and white.
Shadows dance beneath the moon,
In this stillness, hearts attune.

Every creature stirs with grace,
In the quiet, they find their place.
Night unfolds its tranquil charm,
Enfolded safe, we lie, we warm.

From the dusk to dawn's embrace,
Life whispers in this sacred space.
In the stillness, dreams take flight,
Bathed in silver, shining light.

The Light of a Polar Dawn

In the stillness, the morning breaks,
Colors dance on the icy lakes.
A whisper of gold, a tender glow,
Promises of warmth in the crisp, cold snow.

Shadows stretch with the sun's ascent,
Waking dreams that winter lent.
The world adorned in shimmering white,
Awakens softly, kissed by light.

Frosted branches, a glittering sight,
Nature's jewels, pure and bright.
Hearts uplifted, spirits soar,
Together we cherish this dawn once more.

With each breath, the magic stays,
In frozen fields where silence plays.
Underneath the vast, blue dome,
We find in this dawn, a sense of home.

Frigid Reveries

In the quiet of the evening air,
Whispers weave with frosty flair.
Muffled sounds in a world of white,
Each step echoes a soft delight.

Snowflakes dance like fleeting dreams,
Filling the night with gentle gleams.
A canvas stretched, so wide, so free,
Frigid whispers call to me.

Midnight's charm, a silver veil,
Tales of winter in the pale.
Lost in thoughts of days gone by,
As snowflakes swirl and gently sigh.

A spark of warmth, in chill embraced,
Memories linger, softly traced.
Through the hush of frigid night,
I find my heart in silent flight.

Leaves of Frost-kissed Dreams

In the garden where dreams unfurl,
Frost-kissed leaves in a gentle swirl.
Every branch, a story told,
Wrapped in whispers, brave and bold.

Crystals glisten upon the ground,
Nature's magic, beauty found.
The breath of winter, soft and sweet,
Guides us through this frozen retreat.

A tapestry of white and green,
Harmonies within the serene.
In every flake, a dream takes flight,
Leaves of frost dance in the light.

Echoes of laughter, moments shared,
In the frost-kissed air, we've dared.
To weave our hopes in the morning dew,
Each leaf a promise, pure and true.

The Breath of a Snowy Evening

As twilight falls, a blanket deep,
The world in silence, begins to sleep.
Snowflakes drift in the dusky glow,
Wrapping the earth in a shimmering show.

Each breath released, a cloud of cream,
Fleeting moments, like a dream.
Shadows dance 'neath the silver moon,
In winter's grasp, a gentle tune.

Branches bow with a crystal weight,
Nature whispers, "Wait, just wait."
Time slows down as stars appear,
In the snowy night, the heart feels near.

Each snowflake tells a tale of grace,
In this serene, enchanted space.
Together we breathe in the cold,
Wrapped in warmth, our stories unfold.

Portrait of a Shivering Town

In the heart of winter's chill,
Streetlamps flicker, shadows spill.
Silent echoes of the night,
Wrapped in blankets, out of sight.

Windows frost, a breath of dreams,
Curtains drawn, as silence seems.
Footsteps muffled in the snow,
A hushed world, where whispers flow.

Children's laughter fades away,
In the stillness, children play.
Snowflakes dance in soft descent,
Chilling tales of days now spent.

Trees stand bare, their branches creak,
Nature holds its breath, so meek.
Beneath a blanket, everything,
Waits for warmth that spring might bring.

This town shivers, holds its breath,
In frozen peace, it flirts with death.
Each heartbeat wrapped in winter's arms,
A portrait drawn of quiet charms.

Beneath the Icicles' Gaze

Icicles hang like crystal spears,
Guardians of winter's frigid years.
Beneath their gaze, the world stands still,
Each breath is clouded, time does chill.

Snow blankets rooftops, pure and white,
Shadows gather, merging with night.
The moon reflects on icy streams,
Dreams of warmth in frozen themes.

Branches bend with nature's weight,
Hushed whispers from the hands of fate.
Stars peek through the cloudy skies,
Glistening dreams in winter's eyes.

Footprints mark the path we've tread,
In this wonderland, softly spread.
But under icicles, truth remains,
A hint of warmth, as hope sustains.

Beneath the gaze of frozen forms,
Nature weathers all the storms.
In quiet moments, life still flows,
Awaiting spring, where love bestows.

Emissaries of the Snowflakes

Falling softly from the skies,
Whispers of winter's lullabies.
Snowflakes twirl on gentle breeze,
Emissaries with such ease.

Each unique, a fleeting dance,
Captured moments, given chance.
Lands adorned in frosted lace,
Carpets white, a tranquil space.

Nature resting, dreams unfold,
In the chill, the earth makes bold.
Embraced by winter's tender grip,
Every flake, a silent sip.

Chill descends on every street,
Life slows down, a gentle beat.
In this season's softest quilt,
Each bit of magic seems to tilt.

Emissaries, pure and bright,
Reveal the world's forgotten light.
In each fall, a story spun,
Winter's tales have just begun.

Hibernal Stillness

In hibernal stillness, life suspends,
Echoes linger where the snow descends.
Quiet whispers fill the air,
Secrets held with golden care.

Bare trees stretch against the gray,
In solitude, they find their way.
Morning light is pale and thin,
A promise waits, where warmth begins.

Animals dream in their hidden dens,
Wrapped in slumber, time extends.
Under layers, life's pulse remains,
In the cold, a warmth retains.

The world seems paused, a gentle pause,
To reflect on nature's silent laws.
Hibernal calm, a soothing balm,
In the stillness, there's a charm.

As snowflakes frolic in the air,
A tranquil spell beyond compare.
Time will bend, the season's end,
Awakening, as life ascends.

Silent Snowfall

Gentle whispers fill the air,
As flakes dance softly, unaware.
Each one unique, a fleeting grace,
Cloaking the earth in a white lace.

The world holds its breath, serene,
Under a blanket pure and clean.
Trees wear their coats, tall and bright,
In the embrace of soft, quiet night.

Footsteps muffled, the night unfolds,
Stories captured that snow beholds.
Each moment precious, yet so small,
In the gentle hush of silent fall.

The stars peek down through clouds above,
Winking at the peace they love.
Time seems to pause, a tranquil sight,
In the magic of the winter night.

Snowflakes swirling, dreams take flight,
Finding solace in the soft light.
In the stillness, hearts find home,
Where winter's wonders freely roam.

The Chill of Dusk

The sun dips low, a fiery glance,
Casting shadows, a last dance.
Cold air whispers in the trees,
Lifting spirits with a breeze.

Orange hues fade into gray,
As twilight steals the light away.
Stars awaken one by one,
A hint of magic has begun.

Crisp leaves crunch beneath the feet,
The world wrapped in a cooling sheet.
Fires crackle, warmth in the dark,
While nature hums its evening lark.

A silhouette against the sky,
Seeking solace, aiming high.
The chill carries stories untold,
In the embrace of dusk, so bold.

Moonlight gathers, shadows blend,
As day bids night its gentle end.
In this quiet, hearts can heal,
The chill of dusk, a peaceful reel.

Crystal Dreams

In the quiet of the night,
Dreams take flight, a wondrous sight.
Whispers shimmer like the stars,
Carried softly, near and far.

Crystal visions, pure and bright,
Twinkling softly in moonlight.
Each thought a bead, a precious stone,
Crafting realms where hopes are grown.

Through the fog of slumber's veil,
They weave a tapestry, not frail.
Moments captured, sweet and rare,
Floating softly in the air.

A land where wishes breathe and bloom,
Filled with laughter, joy, and room.
In the heart, they're meant to stay,
Guiding souls at break of day.

When dawn awakens, dreams may flee,
Yet their spark stays within me.
In the light, they shimmer still,
Crystal dreams that time can't kill.

Winter's Embrace

Frost-kissed mornings greet the dawn,
In winter's arms, the world is drawn.
Each breath a plume, soft and white,
Warming hearts in the chilly night.

Icicles dangle, glistening fair,
Nature's jewels, beyond compare.
A blanket of snow muffles sound,
In winter's hug, peace is found.

Children's laughter fills the air,
As they tumble without a care.
Joyous echoes, bright and clear,
In winter's world, love is near.

The nights grow long, the stars shine bright,
Guiding dreams into the night.
In every flake, a story sleeps,
As the world in quietness keeps.

With every season's soft goodbye,
Winter whispers, low and shy.
In her embrace, we find our grace,
A moment cherished, time and space.

Dreams in White

In a world so pure and bright,
Snowflakes dance in gentle flight.
Soft blankets cover all we see,
Whispers of a winter's glee.

Children laugh as snowballs fly,
Underneath the azure sky.
Frosty breaths fill the air,
As joy remains without a care.

Footprints trace a winding path,
In this realm of frosty math.
Snowman smiles with carrot nose,
As warmth in hearts continually grows.

Dreams awaken with the dawn,
In the hush, our hopes are drawn.
Imagination, free to roam,
In winter's chill, we find our home.

As evening falls, stars appear,
Guiding dreams that feel so near.
Wrapped in blankets, hugs so tight,
We drift softly into night.

Charmed by Icicles

Icicles hang like crystal spears,
Glistening bright as winter nears.
A silent magic fills the air,
Charmed by beauty, beyond compare.

Branches heavy with frozen grace,
Nature's artwork, a brilliant lace.
Every drip is a song unsung,
From the edges, where ice is hung.

Sunlight breaks on frosty morn,
Painting hues of pale and worn.
A dance of light, a shimmered play,
Casting shadows as children sway.

Winds whisper secrets through the trees,
In the crisp, they hum like bees.
Joyful hearts skip like a stone,
In frosted realms, we're never alone.

As twilight drapes a velvet sheet,
Icicles sparkle, bittersweet.
Underneath the starlit skies,
Winter's charm forever lies.

Nurtured by the Chill

In the cold, we find our fire,
Nurtured dreams, our one desire.
Breath of winter wraps us tight,
Cozy moments, pure delight.

Fires crackle in the night,
Gathered close, warmth feels right.
Hot cocoa shared with laughter,
Memories crafted, ever after.

The world outside is draped in white,
Nature's canvas, pure and bright.
Snowflakes fall like whispered tales,
In this land where magic prevails.

Each gust brings a frosty kiss,
In our hearts, we find our bliss.
Playing games beneath the sky,
With winter's chill, we laugh and fly.

As seasons change and time rolls on,
We hold the chill, forever drawn.
In the embrace of icy grace,
We find our home, our sacred space.

Whispers of the Sky

Clouds gather, shades of gray,
Whispers of the sky hold sway.
A soft murmur, a gentle sigh,
Promises danced in breezes high.

Raindrops fall like silver tears,
Washing dreams, quieting fears.
In the storm's melodic song,
We find a place where we belong.

Sunlight breaks, a golden thread,
Weaving warmth where hope is fed.
Beneath the arcs of fading light,
We chase the shadows of the night.

Stars emerge, glimmering bright,
Guiding souls through velvet night.
Every twinkle, a story told,
Whispers of dreams, brave and bold.

The sky, a canvas vast and wide,
Holds our secrets, in clouds they hide.
With every breath, we glance above,
Finding peace, and endless love.

Chill of the Whispering Breeze

The breeze it whispers soft and low,
A tale of winter's gentle woe.
Through barren branches, it sweeps and sighs,
A lonesome echo under gray skies.

It dances past the frozen streams,
Where shadows linger, lost in dreams.
A chill that bites, yet stirs the heart,
Reminding us that warmth will start.

With every gust, the secrets flow,
Of silent nights and moonlit glow.
In every breath, the world stands still,
Awash in peace, a quiet thrill.

The leaves may rustle, yet they freeze,
Caught in the chill of whispering breeze.
A fleeting moment, soft and vast,
A timeless song from winters past.

Frosted Veils of Silence

Frosted veils drape over the land,
A white embrace, so soft and grand.
Silence blankets every sound,
As nature sleeps beneath the ground.

Every branch adorned in white,
Glistens softly in the night.
Under stars, so bright and clear,
Whispers linger, drawing near.

Footprints vanish, lost to time,
In this realm, so pure, sublime.
Moments freeze, yet hearts ignite,
In the depths of winter's night.

The world wrapped in this frosted glow,
Holds a beauty, soft and slow.
Veils of silence, still they stay,
Guarding secrets of the day.

Through the twilight, dreams arise,
In frosted veils, the spirit flies.
To wander through this magic scene,
Where everything is pure and clean.

Crystalline Dreams in the Night

In crystalline dreams of the night,
Stars cascade with shimmering light.
Each twinkle spins a tale unspun,
Of midnight journeys and days begun.

Soft whispers drift on silver air,
A serenade beyond compare.
Night blooms gently with each soft sigh,
As shadows dance beneath the sky.

In this realm where silence thrives,
Awakens magic, where hope derives.
The cool embrace, a soothing balm,
Finds every heartbeat, still and calm.

With elegance, the moon's bright gaze,
Illuminates the hidden ways.
Crystalline dreams weave through the dark,
Igniting sparks with every arc.

Together in the quiet, we roam,
Finding solace, our secret home.
In the depths of night, our dreams take flight,
In crystalline wonders, pure delight.

A Shiver's Embrace

A shiver's embrace, winter's kiss,
Wraps the world in icy bliss.
With every breath, the air confides,
Stories held where stillness abides.

Frosted whispers trace the ground,
In this hush, a peace is found.
Moments linger beyond the dawn,
As nature waits, the past withdrawn.

In shadows where the cold winds weave,
Hope's soft glow we still believe.
A dance of chills, the heart's delight,
Brings warmth alive in the frozen night.

Beneath the stars, the dreamers stroll,
Wrapped in night, we feel it whole.
With every shiver, joy's embrace,
A tender bond we cannot replace.

Through starlit paths, our spirits soar,
In winter's arms, forever more.
The world may chill, yet love inspires,
A flame that warms through frozen fires.

Frost-Kissed Reflections

In the dawn's soft glow, still and bright,
Frost-kissed trees gleam, a stunning sight.
Mirrors of nature, ice-clad and grand,
Whispers of winter across the land.

Footprints linger, secrets held tight,
In the crunching snow, echoes ignite.
Beauty in stillness, a chill in the air,
Nature's serenity, beyond compare.

Sparkling crystals, delicate lace,
Every breath fogs in the chilly space.
Sunlight dances on surfaces rare,
Frost-kissed moments, precious to share.

Seasons blend in this winter's grace,
Time slows down at a gentle pace.
Reflections of memories etched in white,
Holding the warmth of a heart's delight.

As day turns to dusk, colors ignite,
The sunset casts shadows, a fading light.
Frost-kissed reflections, a tale retold,
A canvas of beauty, a sight to behold.

Beneath the Icy Veil

Beneath the icy veil, secrets lie,
Whispers of dreams drift quietly by.
A world transformed in cold embrace,
Nature's wonder, a mystical space.

Glistening shadows, a haunting sight,
Stars twinkle softly in the still night.
The moonlight bathes the snow in glow,
Footsteps echo where few dare go.

Silent stories in each frozen stream,
Time itself pauses, a gentle dream.
Old trees stand guard in their white coats,
A quiet reverie, the heart promotes.

In this realm where cold winds sigh,
Hope flickers softly, a warm reply.
Underneath the blanket of frost so pale,
Life stirs gently, beneath the icy veil.

As shadows lengthen and daylight fades,
Nature holds on, its beauty pervades.
With every heartbeat, a melody flows,
In harmony soft, where the cold wind blows.

Quietude of the Season

In winter's grasp, a hush envelops all,
Nature whispers softly, a muted call.
The world rests still in this serene embrace,
Quietude of the season, a sacred space.

Snowflakes drift like whispers from above,
Layering earth with a blanket of love.
Trees stand tall, adorned in purest white,
Guardians of silence in the fading light.

Footsteps muffled in the powdered snow,
Echoes of moments, where soft winds blow.
Each breath leaves markings in the crisp air,
Fleeting reminders of winter's care.

Stars blink brightly in the velvet sky,
Bathe the silence, a lullaby.
The night holds secrets, tranquil and true,
Quietude of the season, a gentle view.

As dawn awakens, a blush on the land,
The beauty of stillness by nature's hand.
In the heart of winter, we pause to find,
Peace lies waiting, serene and kind.

Frozen Echoes

Frozen echoes of laughter long past,
Dance in the silence, shadows they cast.
Memories linger in crystal and frost,
In a world where warmth feels almost lost.

Time trickles slowly in the winter's sigh,
Whispers resound as the cold winds cry.
Each flake tells a story, unique and true,
In the tapestry woven by icy hue.

The golden sun dips, a farewell so bright,
Painting the sky in a blend of twilight.
Frosted landscapes shimmer and glow,
A moment held dear, in a world of snow.

Listen closely to the tales that it brings,
Frozen echoes, the melody sings.
In the stillness, joy finds its place,
Cocooned in winter's comforting embrace.

As nightfall descends, stars begin to shine,
Guiding our thoughts to the divine.
Frozen echoes, sweet time to reflect,
In the heart of winter, we deeply connect.

Blue-Hued Fantasies

In a realm of azure skies,
Dreams take flight like butterflies,
Whispers dance on ocean's wave,
Painting thoughts we long to crave.

Stars align in sapphire night,
Guiding hearts in gentle light,
Echoes of a lullaby,
Filling spaces, oh so shy.

Mountains draped in cerulean,
Calling forth the wildest dreams,
Where imagination roams free,
And we touch eternity.

Waves of cobalt sweep the shore,
Crashing chords, a timeless score,
In this world of endless blue,
All our fantasies come true.

Let us paint with twilight's brush,
In the quiet, feel the rush,
Of blue-hued fantasies untold,
In our hearts, forever bold.

Candles in the Cold

Flickering lights in winter's breath,
Casting warmth amidst the death,
Candles glow, a soft embrace,
In the night, we find our place.

Shadows dance on walls of white,
Echoes linger in the night,
Stories told by golden flame,
Whispers gently call our name.

Frosted windows, scenes unfold,
Every spark a tale retold,
Huddled close, we share and dream,
In the glow, love's subtle gleam.

Through the chill, our hearts ignite,
Candles shine, a beacon bright,
In the stillness, hope takes hold,
Against the dark, brave and bold.

Let the winter winds blow wild,
We remain, resilient, styled,
With candles in the cold, we sing,
Turning frost to warmth, our wing.

Icebound Reverie

Amidst the frost, where silence reigns,
Time stands still, as beauty wanes,
Crystal shards on branches cling,
Nature's breath a whispering.

Dreams ensnared in winter's light,
Glimmers shine through the cold night,
Every flake, a magic trace,
Ethereal in this frozen space.

In the still, we weave our dreams,
Flowing softly like moonbeams,
Carried on the icy breeze,
Dancing softly, hearts at ease.

Stillness holds the world in sway,
In this deep, where shadows play,
Moments linger, sweet and rare,
In the silence, love laid bare.

Icebound reveries, pure and bright,
We find solace in the night,
Embracing all that winter gives,
In this realm, our spirit lives.

Solstice Serenade

Beneath the ancient winter sky,
The solstice sings a mellow sigh,
In the dark, the light will grow,
As seeds of hope begin to sow.

Voices rise in harmony,
Nature's song, a symphony,
Rejoicing in the coming sun,
Celebrating all that's yet to come.

Candles flicker, shadows play,
Guiding us along the way,
In the chill, we find our peace,
As love's warm glow will never cease.

The night dances with vibrant star,
Leading souls both near and far,
In the stillness, hearts align,
Brightening the ties that bind.

In the pause before the dawn,
All our worries gently gone,
A solstice serenade begins,
With every note, new life spins.

Ethereal Flurries

Whispers float through the night air,
Softly touching the bare trees.
Snowflakes dance without a care,
In a ballet of gentle breeze.

Silvery light on the ground,
Each flake a jewel, a gift.
Silence wrapped all around,
In nature's soothing shift.

A fleeting moment captured,
Time drifts in this winter scene.
Hearts warmed, though the cold's fractured,
By the magic of what's unseen.

Every breath, a cloud of white,
Echoes of laughter in the chill.
Through the stillness, pure delight,
As snowflakes fall, they gently thrill.

In the morning, a blanket vast,
Covering all in quiet grace.
Ethereal flurries, fading fast,
A fleeting dream in this space.

The Moonlight's Freeze

Under the gaze of the pale moon,
Every shadow starts to glide.
The night hums a soft tune,
In its chill, we abide.

Reflecting on mirrored lakes,
Stars shimmer in the stillness.
A magic that softly wakes,
Creating a sense of thrillness.

Frosted whispers, crisp and bright,
Each breath hangs in the air.
Wrapped in the cloak of night,
Unraveling dreams laid bare.

Paths illuminated, shadows stretch,
The world feels both close and far.
Beneath the moon's quiet fetch,
We find peace in its star.

Layers of mist drift and weave,
Kissing the ground, a soft tease.
In the night, we believe,
In the magic of moonlit freeze.

Shadows of North Winds

From mountains high, the cold winds blow,
Carving whispers through the trees.
They dance and twist, a haunting show,
In tune with the winter's freeze.

A hush falls deep, the world holds breath,
Echoes of past seasons fade.
The north winds bring a touch of death,
Yet life in its silence is made.

Footsteps crunch on frost-kissed ground,
Each step a note in a song.
Nature's symphony surrounds,
In shadows where we belong.

Brittle branches bow in grace,
A tapestry of the night.
In this place, the human race,
Finds solace in the twilight.

North winds whisper tales of old,
Reminders of battles fought.
In their shadows, stories unfold,
In the quiet, we are caught.

Veils of Silence

In the depths of twilight's hush,
Wrapped in veils of silence deep.
Where thoughts wander, and hearts rush,
In dreams, the world takes a leap.

The quiet speaks in gentle tones,
Each whisper a promise of peace.
A place where time's essence condones,
Letting all troubles release.

Veils of mist hug the ground tight,
Embracing all in soft embrace.
Stars twinkle, painting the night,
In their glow, we find our place.

Every breath, a moment captured,
Fleeting like whispers of air.
In silence, our souls are raptured,
Floating high without a care.

When dawn breaks, the veils will lift,
Revealing the world with a sigh.
But in silence, we found the gift,
In the stillness, we learn to fly.

A Glistening Tale

In the morning light so bright,
Dreams take flight, a joyful sight.
Whispers of hope on the breeze,
Glistening tales among the trees.

Each leaf a story, each branch a song,
Nature's essence, where we belong.
Rivers sparkle, reflecting the sky,
Carrying secrets as they pass by.

Mountains stand tall, with crowns of snow,
Guardians of memories, they bestow.
In twilight's embrace, shadows dance,
A glistening tale of chance romance.

Beneath the stars, the night unfolds,
A universe wrapped in silver and gold.
Time stands still in this endless maze,
As we weave our hopes in the starlit gaze.

The land whispers softly, a gentle tune,
Inviting us closer, under the moon.
Together we'll wander, hand in hand,
Living this glistening tale so grand.

The Hidden Lull

In quiet corners, dreams will weave,
A hidden lull, where hearts believe.
Underneath the cloak of night,
Whispers call in soft twilight.

Softly spoken, secrets flow,
In the stillness, feelings grow.
Each star a promise, twinkling bright,
Guiding us through the endless night.

A peaceful hush upon the ground,
In this calm, solace is found.
Time drifts slowly, breaths align,
Embracing the magic, truly divine.

In shadows deep, we find our bliss,
Wrapped in dreams, in moments like this.
The world fades away in gentle light,
As we rest easy, through the night.

And when dawn breaks, soft and clear,
The hidden lull will disappear.
Yet in our hearts, it softly glows,
A whispered love that ever flows.

Secrets of the Frost

Morning dew on emerald blades,
Whispers of winter in delicate shades.
Each crystal formed, a tale unfurled,
Secrets of frost, a magical world.

A blanket white over fields so wide,
Hiding treasures that time can't hide.
The crisp air carries a chilled embrace,
Inviting wanderers to this serene space.

Snowflakes dance, a ballet divine,
Each a marvel, a fleeting sign.
They touch the earth with gentle grace,
Painting landscapes, a snowy lace.

Beneath the surface, life persists,
In frozen realms where warmth exists.
Whispers untold in the quiet air,
Secrets of the frost, beyond compare.

As sunlight breaks on a new day's dawn,
The chilly veil slowly is drawn.
Yet traces remain, a ghostly frost,
In memories cherished, never lost.

Starlit Serenity

Under the blanket of a velvet night,
Stars twinkle softly, a beautiful sight.
Whispers of dreams in the moon's warm glow,
Starlit serenity, a gentle flow.

Each star a wish, a moment we share,
Carried on breezes, light as air.
In this hush, our hearts converse,
Bound by the cosmos, a tender verse.

The universe sings in melodious rhyme,
In this stillness, transcending time.
Peace wraps around like a tranquil sea,
As we embrace this harmony.

Beneath the heavens, where silence reigns,
We dance with shadows, release our chains.
In the depths of night, we find our way,
With starlit serenity leading the way.

As dawn approaches, its golden hue,
We carry the night, and all it imbues.
In the light of day, we'll treasure still,
The magic of night, the starlit thrill.

Frostbitten Memories

In the chill of winter's breath,
Silent echoes linger near,
Frozen whispers, tales of death,
Stories wrapped in frosty spear.

Footprints lost in snow's embrace,
Memories drift beneath the haze,
A time once bright, now scarred and traced,
Fading fast in winter's maze.

Yet within this icy grip,
Lies a warmth that can't be quelled,
As I hold each memory's tip,
In my heart, their tales upheld.

Beneath the frost, a fire glows,
A spark of life in barren land,
Through the cold, resilience grows,
In memories, I take my stand.

So I walk this bitter land,
With each step, I gather close,
Frostbitten, but unbroken, I stand,
Cherishing what winter supposed.

Clearing the Crystal Path

A path of ice and silver gleams,
Underneath the frosty morn,
Nature's canvas, wild and dreams,
In every step, the earth is reborn.

Snowflakes dance from heavens high,
Creating patterns on the way,
As I breathe a frosty sigh,
And welcome in the winter's day.

Each crystal shard, a story told,
Of seasons passed, both young and old,
With every shimmer, wisdom's gold,
I walk the dreamland, brave and bold.

Nature whispers in the breeze,
Telling tales of past and future,
With every rustle through the trees,
My heart learns, and I become a tutor.

Thus I tread this crystal path,
With careful grace, through snow and frost,
In every moment, there's a wrath,
Yet beauty found, it won't be lost.

The Emissary of Winter

From the skies, the snowflakes drift,
Heralds sent on winter's breath,
A soft and cold, enchanting gift,
In silence born, a dance with death.

The emissary cloaked in white,
With icy fingers traces lines,
Painting landscapes with sheer delight,
In frozen hours, the world shines.

He whispers secrets to the night,
With moonlight dancing on the snow,
A luminous and ghostly light,
While stars above put on a show.

Amidst the chill, a heart beats strong,
Defying cold with dreams anew,
For even here, where I belong,
The warmth of life will see me through.

As dawn breaks over winter's reign,
The emissary bids farewell,
Yet in my heart, he'll still remain,
A quiet force, a timeless spell.

Silver Solitude

In the stillness of the night,
Silver shadows gently play,
Wrapped in dreams, a pure delight,
In solitude, I find my way.

Moonbeams cast their gentle glow,
Whispering secrets of the past,
Each breath taken, soft and slow,
In silence, healing comes at last.

A world transformed by winter's hand,
Where solitude does find its peace,
Listening to the crystal band,
In grace, my worries find release.

With every flake that tumbles down,
I gather strength from nature's art,
In this vast, embracing gown,
I stitch the pieces of my heart.

So I bask in silver's glow,
A tranquil space where I belong,
In solitude, my spirit flows,
A quiet hymn, a winter song.

The Lullaby of Snow

Whispers fall from skies above,
A blanket soft, a gentle shove.
The world is hushed, no sounds betray,
As snowflakes dance and drift away.

Each flake a dream, a fleeting sigh,
In silver light, they float and fly.
A lullaby for hearts to share,
In winter's grasp, so pure and rare.

The trees stand tall in quiet grace,
A frosted veil, a timeless space.
As night unfolds, the stars ignite,
A symphony of soft moonlight.

With every breath, a cloud ascends,
The chilled embrace, where silence mends.
In this soft haven, we find peace,
As winter's song will never cease.

So close your eyes and drift away,
To realms where dreams and snowflakes play.
In this sweet hush, let worries go,
Embrace the warmth of lullaby snow.

Beneath the Glistening Crust

Beneath the shimmer, secrets lie,
A crystal veil of winter's sigh.
The earth is wrapped in frosty dreams,
Where sunlight glints and softly beams.

Footsteps crunch on icy ground,
Awakening the silence found.
Each icy shard, a tale to tell,
Of seasons past, in winter's spell.

As shadows creep and daylight wanes,
The world transforms, as beauty reigns.
A tranquil realm, so pure, so bright,
Beneath the glistening, soft moonlight.

The whispers through the frosted trees,
A breath of life upon the breeze.
In this white cocoon, we will roam,
Finding warmth in nature's home.

So take my hand, let's wander slow,
Through dreams of white, and heartbeats glow.
We'll chase the dusk till stars align,
Beneath the crust, our souls entwine.

Silent Footfalls

Through the woods where shadows play,
Silent footfalls mark the way.
Each step a whisper, softly tread,
In a world where dreams are fed.

Footprints vanish in the snow,
As if the earth does not want to know.
The stillness wraps around us tight,
A blanket soft, enfolding night.

The air is crisp, the stars are near,
A cosmic dance, both bright and clear.
We move with grace, like ghosts in time,
In this serene and frozen climb.

Branches creak and softly sway,
In the night's embrace where shadows play.
Each silent footfall, a gentle sound,
A melody where peace is found.

So let us walk through winter's maze,
Where every moment swirls and sways.
In this quiet, we find our song,
As silent footfalls lead us along.

The Language of Cold

In whispers soft, the cold speaks true,
To those who pause, and listen through.
A language formed of frost and ice,
Fluent in silence, sweet and precise.

It tells of nights wrapped in white,
Of starlit skies that feel so bright.
Of winter's breath upon your skin,
A chill that sparks the warmth within.

Each flake that falls, a tale to weave,
Of memories held and hearts that grieve.
In frozen moments, time will stand,
A canvas painted by nature's hand.

The world turns slow, as if in dream,
While time cascades like a silver stream.
In echoes of laughter, hearts unfold,
As we embrace the language of cold.

So gather close, and let us share,
The secrets whispered in the air.
In this stillness, let our souls be bold,
As we converse in the language of cold.

Celestial Frost on Earth

In the stillness of the night,
Stars glimmer with icy light.
Ground adorned in white lace,
Nature's soft, cold embrace.

Moonbeams dance on frozen streams,
Whispering secrets, silent dreams.
Trees wear coats of shimmering frost,
Every breath marked, beauty embossed.

Fields of silver, silent sighs,
Beneath the vast, expansive skies.
A world transformed, pure and bright,
In the tranquil, starry night.

Gentle winds make shadows play,
As frost creeps slowly, day by day.
A crystal blanket, pure and true,
In the cold, the world feels new.

The dawn arrives, with hues so bold,
Painting warmth in shades of gold.
Yet the magic still remains,
In the frost, the beauty reigns.

Beyond the Frozen Threshold

A wooden door, a creaking sound,
Leads to wonders yet unbound.
Frozen landscapes, tales untold,
Await the brave, the hearts so bold.

Softly calling from afar,
The glittering frost, a guiding star.
Step through shadows, leave the warm,
Embrace the chill, feel the charm.

Footprints trace where none have been,
In this realm of silver sheen.
Silence sings a haunting tune,
Beneath the gaze of the pale moon.

Swaying branches, a frosted dance,
Whispers of nature's sweet romance.
Underneath the icy veils,
Echoes of forgotten trails.

Vistas stretch, vast and deep,
In every corner, secrets sleep.
Beyond the threshold, worlds collide,
In winter's arms, dreams reside.

Whispering Pines of the Cold

Among the pines, soft breezes sigh,
Whispering tales as seasons fly.
Covered in frost, their needles shine,
Guardians of secrets, old and divine.

Echoes dance on winter nights,
Nature's breath, with frosty delights.
Adorned in snow, standing so tall,
In their presence, you feel the call.

Footsteps crunch on a snowy path,
The trees stand witness, hold their wrath.
In every rustle, stories unfold,
In the woods, the mysteries hold.

Branches sway with grace and might,
Under the blanket of soft moonlight.
Pinecones drop, their secrets spread,
Whispers of life, in silence bred.

Together they stand, in winter's song,
A chorus of nature, wild and strong.
The whispering pines, a soothing balm,
In their embrace, the world feels calm.

The North Wind's Song

The north wind blows, a chilling breath,
Carrying whispers of ancient death.
Through barren trees, it weaves along,
A haunting tune, the north wind's song.

Snowflakes gather, swirling in air,
A ballet of white, dancing with flair.
In the quiet, you can hear,
The echoes of winter, crisp and clear.

Mountains rise, clad in white,
Guardians under the stars' light.
From the heights, the soft winds call,
As night enfolds, the shadows fall.

Frozen lakes, a mirror of dreams,
Reflecting the starlit beams.
Listen closely, feel the sway,
The north wind sings, a lullaby play.

So embrace the chill, the wild, the bold,
In winter's arms, new stories are told.
For in the frost, in every chill,
The north wind's song, forever will.

The Melody of Snowfall

Whispers of snowflakes glide,
A gentle dance on winter's breath.
Each one a delicate surprise,
Falling softly, stilling death.

Chill in the air, a crisp embrace,
Nature's quilt, pure and white.
Songs of silence find their place,
Under the stars, in the night.

Branches bow with snowy grace,
Carpets of frost beneath our feet.
Echoes linger in this space,
Where time and memory meet.

Warmth of hearth in contrast found,
Against the cold, we gather near.
Hearts embraced, no sorrow's sound,
In this magic crystal clear.

So let the world outside freeze tight,
In every flake, a gentle art.
The melody of winter's light,
Plays on the strings of every heart.

Echoes of a Frozen Horizon

Frozen whispers in the breeze,
Silent tales that nature tells.
Beneath the weight of icy trees,
Where winter's spell of stillness dwells.

Footsteps crunch on frosted ground,
A world wrapped in glacial breath.
In this purity, peace is found,
Among the shadows of gentle death.

Horizons stretch in silver hues,
Dimming light, as day does flee.
Each moment hints at twilight's muse,
Wonders lost in reverie.

Yet in the chill, warmth is born,
As dreams take flight on flurry's wing.
From every heart, a hope is worn,
In echoes sweet, the frost does sing.

So linger here, in twilight's glow,
Where cold and warmth embrace as one.
In frozen realms, the winds will blow,
As echoes of this night are done.

Frostbitten Hours

Hours pass in a frosty trance,
The clock ticks slow, in silver sheen.
Each minute holds a precious chance,
To savor quiet, thoughtful scenes.

Outside, the world is clad in white,
Branches dance with icy lace.
The moon casts down its gentle light,
Illuminating nature's grace.

Amidst the frost, we share our dreams,
Wrapped in warmth, two hearts entwined.
Time drips like icicles in streams,
With every breath, our thoughts aligned.

Frostbitten moments, soft and rare,
Seep into the fabric of night.
We linger in this frozen air,
Together, chasing fading light.

So hold me close, as shadows grow,
Within these hours, we are free.
In frostbitten love, we surely know,
The warmth of our shared reverie.

The Stillness of Icebound Souls

In the stillness, shadows flare,
Icebound souls in whispered sighs.
Time stands still in this frozen air,
Underneath the vast, pale skies.

Stillness weaves a tender spell,
Each heartbeat echoes soft and low.
In frozen silence, all is well,
In still water, the calm will grow.

Moments captured, suspended here,
A gallery of winter's grace.
In quietude, we persevere,
Facing the chill of nature's face.

Those icebound souls in moments freeze,
Yet warmth resides within the heart.
Among the snow, we find our peace,
In stillness, never drift apart.

So let us breathe this crisp night air,
And dance beneath the glistening moon.
In the stillness, we lay bare,
Our love, a timeless winter tune.

Twilight in a Frosted Glade

In twilight's embrace, shadows play,
Soft whispers drift, as night sways.
Frosted leaves glimmer, a silvery sheen,
Nature's dreamscape, serene and pristine.

Branches entwined in the cooling mist,
Stars awaken in the twilight's twist.
The moon rises high, casting soft light,
While the world sighs, ready for night.

A hush falls gently, the earth holds its breath,
In the quiet of dusk, life dances with death.
Crickets sing softly, the breeze joins the tune,
Under the gaze of the watchful moon.

Frosted glades shimmer, an enchanting sight,
Echoes of wonder, shimmering bright.
A pathway unfolds through the silver glow,
Leading to secrets the night may bestow.

In this frosted haven, time drifts away,
Wrapped in the magic of twilight's display.
With each fleeting moment, the heart finds its place,
In the stillness of night, a warm, gentle space.

Glistening Footprints

In the morning light, footprints appear,
Leading me onward, crystal clear.
Each step a story, etched in the frost,
Of moments remembered, and time that was lost.

Under bright skies, the world glows anew,
Nature's soft blanket, a shimmering hue.
Whispers of wonder in each chilly stride,
Carrying dreams where warm memories hide.

The echo of laughter lingers in air,
As I traverse paths, the wild to share.
The glisten of snowflakes dances with glee,
Creating a map, guiding me free.

Every glistening footprint tells of my day,
Marking adventures in the snow's bright array.
A tapestry woven of joy and delight,
In the heart of winter, all feels so right.

As dusk approaches, the footprints may fade,
But within my heart, those memories stayed.
Glistening depictions of moments well spent,
Chasing the magic, wherever time lent.

The Quietude of Frosted Mornings

Frosted mornings quietly unfold,
A world wrapped in white, tranquil and bold.
Whispers of winter, soft and serene,
Nature adorned in a shimmering sheen.

Breath of fresh air, crisp with delight,
Glistening crystals sparkle in light.
Each frozen branch waves in the breeze,
A symphony played through the rustling leaves.

Soft footsteps echo on the glistening ground,
In the embrace of the quiet, peace found.
Hints of a sunrise, painting the skies,
A canvas of colors that gently arise.

Silhouettes dance as shadows retreat,
The hush of the morning, oh so sweet.
Time pauses long, wrapped in still grace,
In this frosted haven, a warm, safe space.

As the sun rises, the chill starts to fade,
Yet the magic remains, quietly played.
Frosted mornings, a moment so rare,
A reminder of beauty, the world lays bare.

Breath of the Arctic Moon

Beneath the Arctic moon, the world holds its breath,
An ethereal glow, life dances with death.
Shadows stretch long on a blanket of white,
An enchanting dreamscape, bathed in soft light.

Whispers of winds sing their chilling refrain,
Carving out stories on the frozen plain.
Each snowflake a wonder, vibrant and bright,
Twinkling like stars in the depth of the night.

The stillness surrounds, yet life gently stirs,
In the hush of the wild, the heartbeat occurs.
Creatures drawn forth by the moon's silken glow,
Resting their hopes in the moon's tranquil show.

Under the vastness, hearts beat as one,
The sparkle of frost, the warmth of the sun.
Alluring and bright, the Arctic scene glows,
As the breath of the moon weaves its magic and flows.

Innocence captured in this moonlit trance,
Nature unfolds in a midnight dance.
The hush of the night, the coolness it brings,
Under the Arctic moon, the spirit takes wing.

Harvesting the Cold

Frosted fields lie still,
Harvesters of winter's chill.
Grains wrapped in icy breath,
Glimmers of a quiet death.

Snowflakes fall like whispers,
Blanketing earth, soft shivers.
Barren trees stand stoic, true,
Awaiting spring's warm debut.

In the silence, life breathes slow,
Trusting seeds beneath the snow.
Nature sleeps, a dream unfurled,
Waiting for a green-touched world.

Chill winds sing a haunting song,
In this place where dreams belong.
The moon casts silver on the ground,
In the cold, a solace found.

With every frost, the heart grows wise,
Watching clouds and winter skies.
There's beauty in the still and old,
In every story, harvesting the cold.

Glistening Shadows

In the twilight's gentle haze,
Shadows gleam in silent ways.
Softly dance on frozen streams,
Whispers echo ancient dreams.

Crystals catch the fading light,
Glistening stars in the night.
Each reflection tells a tale,
Of stolen time, of winds that wail.

Amidst the trees, dark and deep,
In this quiet, secrets sleep.
A fleeting glance at what's been lost,
In shimmering, the past embossed.

Beneath the surface, life abides,
In glimmers where mystery hides.
Silhouettes of hopes and fears,
Melt away with unshed tears.

As the dawn begins to glow,
The shadows fade, but beauty grows.
In each glistening, a promise flows,
The warmth awaits where courage goes.

A Dance of Icicles

Hanging from rooftops high,
Icicles gleam against the sky.
A crystal ballet, pure and bright,
Dancing in the silver light.

Dripping secrets from above,
Nature's art born of cold love.
Each drop a note in winter's song,
Echoing where dreams belong.

In the quiet of the night,
Icicles twirl in soft moonlight.
Fragile sculptures, frozen grace,
Nature's beauty, time's embrace.

With every sway, they shimmer low,
Catching fires from earth's warm glow.
Until the sun begins its reign,
Their dance ends with the springtime rain.

In this fleeting, chilly dream,
Life teeters on the frozen beam.
A dance of icicles, time stands still,
In the art of winter's chill.

The Hushed Land

Upon the earth, a soft embrace,
The hushed land speaks in stillness' space.
Muffled whispers fill the air,
In every footstep, love and care.

Trees wear coats of sparkling white,
Guardians of the tranquil night.
Silence cradles all that's near,
Softly held through frost and fear.

Crimson berries pop like gems,
Among the branches where light stems.
Even shadows find their place,
In the quiet, a sacred space.

Snow-draped hills like dreamy sighs,
Underneath the pale blue skies.
The world holds its breath, releases time,
In the hush of winter's rhyme.

As night cloaks the vast expanse,
Stars will spin in a silent dance.
The hushed land, a heartbeat away,
Whispers of hope in shades of gray.

The Silver Cloak of Dusk

The sky transforms to shades of grey,
Whispers of night begin to play.
Stars adorn the velvet expanse,
The moonlight casts a fleeting glance.

The silver cloak wraps all around,
Hushed secrets in the twilight found.
Gentle breezes stir the trees,
As shadows dance with graceful ease.

Creatures pause in evening's hold,
Silent tales of wonder told.
In this calm, the heart finds peace,
A tranquil space where worries cease.

Time slows down with every breath,
In dusk's embrace, we flirt with death.
Hope flickers like a distant star,
Guiding dreams of where we are.

So let the silver cloak enfold,
Our stories whispered, brave and bold.
With every dusk, a new embrace,
The world transformed in twilight's grace.

Beneath the Crystal Canopy

A world adorned in frosty light,
Nature's charm gleams pure and bright.
Trees wear crowns of icy lace,
In this realm, we find our space.

Underneath the crystal sky,
Snowflakes twirl and softly sigh.
Each one dances with delight,
Painting landscapes, pure and white.

Frozen branches gently sway,
Whispering secrets of the day.
Footprints trace a path of dreams,
Beneath the light, the world redeems.

In this hush, the heart can feel,
The quiet strength of winter's reel.
Nature's breath, a gentle hum,
A symphony of peace to come.

So linger here in frosty air,
Beneath the sky, a moment rare.
Encased in beauty, time stands still,
In crystal realms, our spirits thrill.

Respite in the Frost

The dawn breaks with a crystal grin,
Softly painting all that's been.
In winter's grasp, we find our way,
A refuge where our hearts can play.

Snowflakes drift like dreams untold,
Whispers of the night turned gold.
Frosted windows, a warming sight,
Inviting tales of pure delight.

Atop the hill, the silence reigns,
Nature rests, free from its chains.
In this chill, the warmth we share,
Brings forth joy in frosty air.

Let laughter echo in the cold,
In treasured moments, life unfolds.
Wrapped in scarves, we wander far,
In winter's clutch, we find our star.

So take a breath, embrace the frost,
In fleeting time, we count the cost.
Together, under skies so vast,
We find respite, our hearts steadfast.

Nature's Frozen Portrait

A canvas draped in icy sheen,
Nature's beauty, rarely seen.
Brushstrokes of white across the land,
A frozen portrait, softly planned.

Mountains wear their coats of snow,
Graceful outlines in sunlight's glow.
Rivers whisper tales of cold,
As frozen stories start to unfold.

Each branch encased, a work of art,
Nature's touch, pure and smart.
Crisp air bites, yet warms the soul,
In winter's grip, we feel its whole.

The silence sings, a sweet refrain,
In this stillness, we find no pain.
Moments captured, time stands still,
In frozen breath, a lasting thrill.

So look upon this wondrous scene,
Let heartbeats feel what might have been.
In nature's portrait, life anew,
Each icy hue a dream comes true.

Milton Keynes UK
Ingram Content Group UK Ltd.
UKHW010232111224
452348UK00011B/713